RAISING *Royalty*

A 14-day Empowerment Workbook for Mother and Daughter

Teaching Self-Identity, Self-Worth, and Self-Love

TESSA THOMPSON

Copyright © 2019 by Tessa Thompson

All rights reserved. No part of this publication may be shared, reproduced, distributed or transmitted in any form or by any means-electronic, mechanical, digital, photocopy, recording, or any other-except for brief quotations in printed reviews, without prior written permission. Written permission must be secured from the author.

If you would like permission to use material from the book (other than for review purposes), please contact author@mrstessathompson.com. Thank you for your support of the author's rights.

P.O. Box 85582
Racine, WI 53408
www.mrstessathompson.com

Cover photos by: Charles Hamilton

ISBNs: 978-1-7342677-3-0 (workbook)
978-1-7342677-6-1 (ebook)

CONTENTS

Acknowledgements v

Foreword vii

About the Author ix

Introduction xi

Chapter 1   What's the 411? Learning Communication. 1

Chapter 2   Consistency, Routines & Schedules 9

Chapter 3   "Don't talk to me!" Developing a Strategy for Breakdowns. 20

Chapter 4   "Mommy still loves you." The role of unconditional love 32

Chapter 5   Self - Identity - How she fits in 41

Chapter 6   Self-Worth - How she sees herself and Self-Love - Teaching "I love me" first 51

Chapter 7   Final Thoughts 63

Epilogue 65

ACKNOWLEDGEMENTS

For my *Mom*, *Bernadette* for having the courage to say what you didn't do "right" and the resilience to teach great lessons without saying a word.

For my *Husband*, *Curt* for providing me the opportunity to find purpose in the gift of our children.

For my *Grandparents*, *Leonard & Vera* for our private conversations that offer a sounding board for all I am still learning as a woman & mommy.

For my Children: Destiny Nevaeh, Journey Grace, Heaven Vera, & Canaan Leonard for being the calm, the joy and the storm. You fuel my tenacity and bring insight and depth to my vision.

For my *Bonus Children*, *Curt & Charly* for all the moments you have showed us adults that relationship and authentic love is what matters the most.

For my *Best Friend*, *Mary Alice Ward* for all the moments and conversations you empowered me to be a brave and resilient mommy. I miss your voice, laughter, and assurance. Please keep watching over my babies and be their angel. I love and miss you Pookie.

To my *Step-Father*, *Darry* for being present in my life and offering a different perspective on parenting. Your talks, wisdom and conversation taught me patience as a parent.

To my *Sisters: Natasha, Ta-Shai, Darria,* and *Teirra* thank you for loving me and looking to me as a Role-model. Thank you for showing up and always being in the room to support me.

To my *Nieces: Samara, Savannah, Zaniah, Amajie,* and *Kierston* may this workbook inspire you to believe anything is possible. May you always believe the Princess in you is stronger than anything you face. TeTe Mommy loves you.

Tessa Thompson

To *Tammy, C.J.,* and *Eze* thank you for being my Spiritual brothers and sister for almost twenty years! Your support, empowerment and prayers are always felt.

To my #goalfriends for empowering, supporting and keeping our network strong and consistent and holding me accountable to the things I say I am going to do.

For the *Mommy's* and *Women* who believe in bravery. Who offer kudos and tell each other to keep going when we want to give up. For the Women who offer the saved spots at the gym, the hot latte, and beverages after a long day and a simple check-in. This is for US!

FOREWORD

Open communication between mothers and daughters is so critically important. As a pediatrician and public health doctor, I see first hand how devastating it can be when there are barriers to loving communication and mutual respect between mothers and daughters. During childhood and adolescence, the brains of children are rapidly developing. Experiencing adverse childhood experiences like separation of parents, racism, bullying, witnessing violence in the home, neglect, abuse and other similar situations can negatively impact the developing brain. On the other hand, loving and caring relationships with a nurturing adult in their lives can positively impact the developing brain and lead to more positive socioemotional health for their future. I am so excited about this book and the amazing strategies and tools Tessa will be sharing to enhance open communication between mothers and daughters. It was a great pleasure coaching her through this book writing journey and the content she has in the next several pages will definitely be life changing! Tessa has invaluable experience in this area as not only a social worker but incredible mother. Her strategies and tips are practical and impactful. Fostering these relationships are so incredibly important. Thank you for taking the time to read this book and let's continue to work together to empower, love, and support our young ladies!

Dr Jasmine Zapata, MD, MPH
www.DrJasmineZapata.com

ABOUT THE AUTHOR

Tessa Thompson is a proud Veteran of the United States Air Force (Served in Operation Enduring and Iraqi Freedom). Thompson graduated from the University of Wisconsin Parkside with a BA in Sociology and Spanish. She received a Master of Social Work from the University of Wisconsin Milwaukee. She is a Solution Focused and Holistic Perspective Social Worker. Thompson believes in looking at the whole person in their environment and works to empower others by developing a plan to meet future goals. Thompson currently works as a School Social Worker in a high school setting. Thompson is an entrepreneur and founder of Balanced Vision Consulting LLC, a service based agency to empower others to change their narrative and be their best self.

Thompson's greatest joy is her life as wife and mother of six blended children through adoption, marriage and a love story. Their journey can be found at www.blending6.com. She currently resides in Racine, Wisconsin with her family.

INTRODUCTION

If I could choose one word to describe myself, I would say *"empowered."* I am stronger and more confident because of my experience as a mother. I have learned to balance and take control of my life by claiming my vision and walking in it with power. I am a mother of six children; one child I adopted as a single foster mother, two children through marriage and three children that my husband and I both share. I am the eldest of five girls, so I feel like I have been a mother for quite some time. My youngest sister was born when I was in middle school. I am a social worker who has held many challenging yet rewarding opportunities in children and family services, mental health, and substance abuse counseling. I am currently in a position and environment I love as a high school social worker. I have the gift of knowing my purpose and why I am breathing the air I breathe and it is definitely to give my all as a woman who empowers others to be their best self. I enjoy the reward.

I wrote this workbook not because I have all of my adulting, parenting or stuff together, but as a source of empowerment. My youngest child is three years of age, therefore, there is plenty I am still learning. There are infinite areas that cause second guessing with our children. I want to bring strength to the areas that are still not all the way clear. I wanted a space where we could be free to figure it out with them. Free to encourage our daughter's resilience by creating opportunities to communicate in difficult spaces. I want our Princess to be able to trust our word. I want other ways to communicate when she doesn't feel like mommy will understand. I want there to be a track record of our relationship that is tangibly seen, felt and heard. A foundation of "how," - how to communicate and tell me things and not just because we want her to. There is a difference in saying, "You can come talk to me about anything," but then not fostering that communication in ways you both can relate to. I want us (as moms) to have space and created moments of humor, reward, and resilience building.

By definition, a Queen: is the most powerful chess piece that each player has, able to move any number of unobstructed squares in any direction along a rank, file, or diagonal on which it stands. This book is for the cultivation and raising of Royalty. As Queens we are raising our Princesses to look at the world in such a way that nothing is impossible. They maneuver, learn and become resilient because of the lessons we teach, the patience we provide and the listening ear we give as Mothers. Mothers who are fostering, adopting, mentoring, biological, step-mother, God-Mother and the mothers (like me) who may find themselves being a mom even though they didn't ask to be. Also, the moms who stand in the gap and ultimately grow to love and be exactly what is needed.

This workbook is important, because I believe a lot of us give and put expectations on ourselves as mothers. We have an expectation for the Princesses we are raising; yet we rarely receive or provide the "how." In being our child's first teacher, we want to provide the "how" that tears down expectations. We do so by cultivating a relationship where there are no boundaries (in love) when expectations are not met. Our princess (no matter her age) does not feel despair, brokenness, or defeat. Our Princesses speak without fear and judgement. We realize our daughters will always be our little girls and in cultivating this relationship they become the Queens they are destined to be.

This topic is important to me because I didn't have this with my mother. My mother always told me, "I'm not your friend, I'm your mother." It created a barrier to organic conversation and relationship building. I became scared to talk to her about things, other than day to day matters, because I didn't know how she would respond. I vowed I wanted my relationship with my daughters to be different. However, how many of us know we too become our mothers. It was all too telling for me when my teenage daughter told me she didn't want to talk to me about a certain subject. I emphatically reacted by saying, "Who me?!" In my mind, I just knew I was the most open minded person of them all. She was going to get the best social worker and mommy response of her life. Her perspective took me for a whirlwind. As a mother to four Princesses, I knew something needed to change. How would I blend and balance what I learned from my mother (the good and the ingrained), my knowledge in academia, and my personal experience and desires?

In this workbook we will be discussing how to create organic consistency in conversations that-- no matter the time or the place-- even the most difficult conversations can be had. We will utilize tools and discuss strategies for when either one of us do not or should not communicate. We will discuss how to deal with despair, hurt, and the ugly things we don't always want to talk about. Finally, we will empower our Princess with the vital sense of self in self-identity, self-worth, and self-love. These learned strategies will be a foundation of positivity and self-affirmation.

Use this workbook in a manner in which is cathartic for you. There may be a chapter that jumps out to you more than the others, start there. After you've finished a chapter discuss what you've learned with your daughter and journal about your insight. A lot of times we learn new information, have great 'aha' moments, all to never pick them up again. Journal recommendations have been incorporated to provide greater writing prompts, strategies, tools and reflection for you and your Princess. It has been formatted to fourteen days. These days are not meant to be consecutive. Please feel free to start and/or stop where it is comfortable for both you and your Princess. It is okay if you are reflecting on Day 4 – for a week before moving on. There is also space created throughout each chapter for self-reflection and empowerment. Please utilize the space provided in the book as well as purchase the accompanying journal, *Royalty* for greater writing depth when needed.

My vision for you and your daughter once you are done with this workbook is that you will have a "how-to." You will communicate when emotionally you want to breakdown and disengage. A healthy relationship will be born, where there is open communication that is naturally organic and authentic in its nature. Your foundation of building in discussion and conversation topics will create a continued space where topics are discussed over a walk in the park, in the car, while hanging at the mall or even in the living room. When the times are rough there will be no hesitation from either of you to discuss any topic. Because you have created and fostered deeper conversations over time.

With Love,
Tessa

Communication — the imparting or exchanging of information by speaking or writing.

CHAPTER 1

What's the 411? Learning Communication.

In normal adolescence, it is very natural to receive typical one-word responses from our children. I think we know the "Fine…..., I'm good…..., okay…..." all too well; when we were hoping to hear all the juicy details about their first day of school, work, outings and friendships. We tend to feel ourselves prying, as if speaking openly and gushing out all that happened from the morning to the afternoon is told all at one time. We don't notice how the short spurts of speaking may happen organically, while driving in the car, that we have to pay attention to. For example, she starts talking about her new friend as we prepare dinner or the interaction of the classroom on the drive home. Those moments are organic, natural, and unforced. It is in those moments that we will continue to build a foundation of greater conversation. Authentic, trusted communication happens, because we have already been talking! You can't expect to have a conversation about her new boyfriend, the secrets she's keeping or what happened at school, and the only conversation you have is "How was school today?"

Instead of asking "How was your day," I will ask my Princess

_____

_____

_____

Tessa Thompson

> *The Dictionary defines communication as: the imparting or exchanging of information by speaking, writing, or using some other medium. The communication we will be discussing and using as a tool in Raising Royalty is speaking and writing.*

As mothers we speak effortlessly. We rarely have difficulty 'finding the words;' They simply roll off of our tongues and we say what comes to mind. We speak from our experiences. We speak from our heart. Being mindful to tell ourselves to carry restraint when speaking is not always a conscious decision. We want our daughters to know how we feel, what we mean, and how to understand. So, we speak. Writing, on the other hand takes on a skill we have to remind ourselves about, as mothers. We pause and then we write. We say we don't have the time. We wonder who we are writing for? What is the purpose for writing? Will this be shared? We rarely provide a sense of unconscious thinking where our imagination can be our guide.

As adolescent girls write, I have seen imagination, peace and joy. I see freedom with them writing their name in cursive, writing a short story, coloring or enjoying doodling with the latest gel pen colors and mandala book. Free to learn to write; not caring about what it will say or come out to be. In adolescence years with girls, I have seen and heard restraint, only when speaking. Speaking to be able to share their thoughts, questions, intents or fears. Restraint happens because they are unsure. Unsure of what mom will say. How will the words be perceived? Will I be judged? Will I be in trouble? Will she understand? So she is often silenced.

A major barrier to communication is: when the other person does not want to write or speak. Communicating when neither of you are ready or should probably take some space, can be detrimental to any relationship. Forced communication looks like less than 3 to 5 feet in either of your personal spaces. It feels like you are not in control or in a safe space (whether emotionally or physically). You may be unsure of what is going to come next. Forced communication sounds like a scream, yell or cursing. It sounds like anything that would be a release, in that moment, for either person.

In some respects, I must remind us of the authority and respect that comes with communication between a mother and daughter. For most, there is an unspoken respect for mothers that is given AND earned. After all, we are the women who birthed these little humans into the world after carrying them not nine months, but ten! We are constantly reminded that you only get one so treat her with respect. One has to admit we have developed through adolescence to teenage years and remember the awkward years of probably despising the mom you were told to reverent. We thankfully get through puberty and hormonal challenges and realize her for the blessing she is. We celebrate and practice "Mother's Day" more than once a year. Hopefully, we have learned the value and infinite wisdom she possesses while she is still breathing. For all intents and purposes we are now talking about how we are seen by our own daughters who are not yet Queens. We are raising them to be that way and sometimes we do that from a place of authority. We want them to follow our directions and respect what we are communicating. We constantly may ask "What's the matter?" or "What's wrong?" when space should be given. We don't always offer other tools or ways to communicate other than "speaking." We immediately want to solve the problem because we hurt when they hurt and we want what is best for them.

One can overcome the barrier of authoritative communication by, developing other tools and ways to communicate with your Princess. Writing is a tool that can be a release for the both of you. No matter what age your Princess is, whether she is young like my Heaven (at five) or a teenager like my Destiny (at fourteen); my hope is that you will grow through speaking and writing together. It is my hope that in place of authority you will learn and practice mutual respect for one another.

As an adoptive mother, communication with my child was difficult. Even though she came to my home at the age of one and a-half and was adopted at the age of four, a barrier was already created. Learning to communicate through trauma, hurt, and resentment is not easy. By not being a child's biological mother, I thought that would make our relationship more genuine, demonstrate gratitude and a loving appreciation. There were a lot of barriers I was unaware of. The communication between mother and daughter has a lot to do with attachment. This hit me hard through my Master's thesis of Reactive Attachment Disorder and how it will forever affect me and my daughter's communication. If this is something you have ever heard of as a grandparent or family member becomes the parent to children with absent parents, you know the pain it creates. In this book, I will give you some sentence starters and journaling prompts which help us learn to "start over" and "meet each other where we are at."

As Queens we are raising our Princess to look at the world in such a way that nothing is impossible.

Journal Recommendation: Learning Communication

Day 1: Create a **Self-Portrait** with your Princess. Offer colored pencils, gel pens, crayons and other things to accentuate your self-portraits. Provide as much detail as you both would like first individually. And then give an opportunity for each of you to share once completed. If your Princess finds difficulty in creating her self-portrait provide options on the canvas to give her a gentle start. Options could include a face, ears, etc. Provide prompts about where would your ears go? Your eyes? What kind of hair would you draw?

Teaching Self-Identity, Self-Worth, and Self-Love

Journal Recommendation: Learning Communication

Day 2: Discover ways your daughter enjoys being loved by you. Come up with a list of questions of things you already do with your Princess and see which ones she enjoys the most. Be intentional to ensure the one she enjoys the most you create time and opportunity for.

Use the following questions as a guide:

Out of the following things which do you enjoy the most?

- Having an opportunity to cuddle with mom on the couch while having your back or feet rubbed?
- Having mommy time for an hour just me and you while we do an out of home activity.
- Having mommy help you with an arts and crafts project or cooking a meal together?
- Hearing mommy encourage you, and share with others, good things about you?
- Being given a nice gift from mommy?
-
-
-
-
-

My Princess loves when I love her by:

I will be intentional in this area of communication by:

Teaching Self-Identity, Self-Worth, and Self-Love

"Free to learn to write; not caring about what it will say or come out to be.

CHAPTER 2

Consistency, Routines & Schedules

Our American culture teaches us success by routines and schedules. In America early education is begun as soon as three years old. Our children begin pre-school where they learn colors, shapes, the alphabet, eating snacks, and going to the bathroom among other routines. Routines and schedules are something children begin to rely on and learn from. It is taught by our environment and our culture to be consistent, to develop routines and to stick to a schedule. When our children are in spaces where consistency in routines and schedules are lacking it creates an unequal balance.

You probably are doing a lot of routine and consistent things in your home right now that you don't even point out to your children as it is just a part of second nature. Just something everyone in the house is used to. So if I came over and took out that part of your day I know it would create a little bit of chaos in your home. That is what shows you the importance and success of your created schedules and routines. I am in no shape of the word saying your home should be running like a boot camp. Even being a military veteran I do realize that would create stress on our children if they were not free to be their playful, free will learning selves. I am saying there are some things our children should expect to know is routine in our home. Small things such as after dinner they know they have to brush their teeth. They know they get a story before bedtime. They say their prayers before they eat. They pick out their clothes before they go to bed at night. This creates balance and peace for their lives and yours as well. It may be the reason you created the rules, schedule and structure in the first place. If a child never knows what to expect next it can create stressors for them. We want our children to feel safe and loved and to know what is going to come next. It doesn't have to be elaborate it just needs to be intentional.

What are some things you are doing already that have become a consistent routine and schedule for your household? How do those things benefit your family?

_____
_____
_____
_____
_____
_____
_____
_____
_____
_____

THE CONSEQUENCES OF NOT BEING CONSISTENT WITH OUR CHILDREN CREATES A CHAOS THAT SPILLS OVER INTO OTHER ENVIRONMENTS OUTSIDE OF THE HOME. You see temper tantrums, anger, in attentive to tasks they are working on and an overall inability to manage their emotions. Children thrive or do much better in structured activities. Every day I make sure I am doing some type of "structured" activity with the kids and what that simply means is that they have mommy reading a book to them, doing flash cards, or my daughter Journey's favorite is always the craft activities on the weekends. Making slime, or bracelets, playing Legos or monster trucks, coloring with them, journaling with them back and forth. Structured activities are when mommy is not just telling them to go and play or go to work on an activity I am engaged in the activity with them.

As a mom of six children there are many times I can think of when I did not demonstrate consistency with my own children. I have regret and wish I would have kept going with tasks, ideas, or wonderful things I saw and started from Pinterest. Such as new charts or organizational household things. One complete struggle that I do not feel I am alone with as a mom, is food. The ability to be consistent in the foods in our home and my own thought process to establish a routine and schedule has been difficult. Like a lot of new mommy's, I started out absolutely wonderful with my first daughter I adopted as well as my biological daughter. I mean I was, THAT mom who checked all the food labels and when I found out that everything was not organic I bought a ninja and blended foods. I nursed all of my children at least until age one and a half. With my youngest son nursing through age three. I gave healthy options and was very much aware of the foods they ate. Then came the toddler years and me being a mom to two babies! All three of my children are a year and a half apart. So when the babies kept coming it just seemed like I had less and less time and things became even more hectic at the house. Not only that, but preparing healthy meals in less than 30 minutes! I didn't prepare for that. Most of the time I would come home and I would just be tired! Pizza, tacos, and pasta became the family go to. As the oldest daughter who always asked my mom why are we always eating the same things I vowed that my children would not eat the same five meals each week. I would introduce new foods, provide different options for veggies and fruit. That was the plan. Again, how many of us know we too become our mothers! So here I became this guilty mom of no longer offering the same veggies and variety that my toddler received when meals were so easy and could be organically provided from a jar of baby food. The lack of consistency and how it affected me was when this mama prepared the healthiest dinner for my kids and they looked at me in disgust, threw tantrums and demanded they didn't want to eat! They now no longer wanted the cooked carrots they hadn't seen in over a month! They want the junk food and comfort foods I had been preparing because I lacked the consistency over time. Veggies and fruits were no longer routine and scheduled in the meal plan. Easy and accessible for this mommy's long day of work and busy schedule was accommodated by weekly pizza and taco nights. This was a huge eye opener for me as a mom of young children. So I am grateful their taste buds change so much right now and I have the opportunity to continue to reintroduce foods and give them a small portion of each thing. I must say though I am some sous chef and you can still catch me on some nights cooking up a jelly sandwich with no peanut butter for the sandwich eaters and then making cracker and pepperoni sandwiches for the other, and for the older kids I can get them to eat my veggie turkey burgers when I try hard enough. Fruits and veggies are based off of trying something new and still have not made a consistent reappearance in the Thompson household as of yet. Don't judge me, they do eat their vitamins!

What is your organization style for home? Do you find your plan not being a 'plan' some days?

I AM GLAD TO REPORT AN AREA OF A WIN FOR THIS MOMMY. I am an avid reader and my consistency, routine and schedule in this area has done very well for our children. The benefits have been that my children love to read as well. They enjoy being read to. They enjoy getting a book and bringing it to me to curl up in my lap and have some cuddle and mommy time while reading a great book. While they are young it is a time I realize I will never get back and so these are precious times for me. For my oldest daughter even in the midst of her behaviors that have caused her to be in out of home placement her reading and comprehension has never suffered. She is commonly told how smart she is. A lot of her consistent consequences were reading and writing. Reading a book and writing a report about it. It was my one form of punishment for the first and last time I was ever suspended growing up. This was a positive mom moment I re-created. We have created reading routines and schedules with our kids that come in the form of reading a book before bedtime, doing flashcards with word recognition and phonics once a day. They know they must first do some type of reading or word comprehension at least once a day prior to any free time. At school their strongest areas are English, reading, and language comprehension. Their teacher does not have difficulty with getting them to read a book out loud or discuss what they have read. It is a moment they have learned to take pride and joy in. In outside environments we enjoy looking at buildings and saying what the words are on the outside. What the name of stores are or finding new words they have never seen before. This consistency in reading has created a space that is welcoming and consistently talked about in a positive manner because of our routine and schedule.

What is a "mom win" you can think of in providing consistent routine or schedule to your household?

_____

_____

_____

_____

_____

_____

_____

Tessa Thompson

FINDING BALANCE AS A WIFE, MOTHER, PROFESSIONAL, ENTREPRENEUR, AND FRIEND AMONG OTHER TITLES IS A HUGE UNDERTAKING. A lot of times a huge barrier for us as moms is having the ability to manage our time. I always say my family is my first job, but the reality of when I come home from work and am exhausted makes me feel like my family comes second. Managing our time is a huge deal. Having the time to stick with work, schedules and self-care is a big part of our day. The reality is it is just not enough time in the day to fit in everything that we would like to do. You come home and you just want to relax! The busyness of the "mom life" is definitely one of the reasons we have a hard time sticking to a consistent routine and schedule.

One of the things I have learned to master as a mom with 6 children and managing so many other responsibilities is **scheduling my tasks against my time**. I started a for profit business called Balanced Vision Consulting LLC., it is based on the tenets of Spirituality, Self-Care, Family, Finances, Career, and Entrepreneurship. I devote various goal setting tasks in each area to my day. Some days I may be able to give a little more time in one area than I was the day before. I work to ensure however that no one area is left untouched for more than 24 hours. Even if it is thirty minutes to an hour to various tasks that I need to complete. I feel if I can at least get something done in my schedule and then work towards it that is better than nothing. That time ultimately builds up and allows me to see the progress I have been working for. I do have to admit you have to have patience with this skill because a lot of times we want to see things happen instantaneously. However, when you have thirty minutes over time it's not going to give you big results, but you should be happy to see the small success and growth of your goals over time. As a mom having a **list of things accomplished versus things to do** greatly helps me as well. Our jobs never end there is always something that we need to do and I found that a lot of times I had a giant to do list where a lot of the things I didn't get to the day before would roll over to the next day. Therefore, my list of things I've completed gives me the "mom win" I need for motivation. Breaking these tasks down into smaller chunks also helps with placing tasks to time.

Would you prefer a "to do list" or "list of accomplishments?" Why?

___

JOURNALING IS A GREAT WAY TO ESTABLISH CONSISTENCY WITH YOUR PRINCESS BECAUSE IT CREATES AN OPPORTUNITY FOR THEM TO TALK ABOUT THEIR DAY. In the midst of our busyness and lives that may seem like they never stop, journaling lets them know they are important, special and valued. Even if it is for 10 minutes after school or before bedtime. Providing a writing prompt to our children and asking them to write after their day gives them imagination and allows them to find the words when they feel they have none. It creates bravery and a space for self-affirming thoughts and behavior as well. Journaling is an easy way for them to have a routine and know you will communicate back with them. Sometimes I may write back with my daughter and provide comments which become a discussion point during our mommy daughter time. Find what works best for you and your daughter. Develop a special writing place, storage space and even where she would turn the journal in to you. Your consistency is important as you have to determine to ensure you read it daily as well. Make it become your daily bedtime reading book or morning reading leisure. This is an opportunity for you to create a special bond to be cherished for years to come. It is definite to touch more than just your relationship. This will be a foundational life skill that will be demonstrated in many areas of her life as she becomes the Queen she is destined to be.

This is an opportunity for you to create a special bond to be cherished for years to come.

Journal Recommendation: Routines and Schedules

Day 3: Sit with your daughter and come up with a **Journaling Schedule**. Establish a goal together of how and when you will write. What will be your exchange routine? Can you find a special box or place to put your journal in that you both can share?

Why I want to write with you:

Our writing goal:

When we will exchange our journal:

Our special place to keep our Journal:

Teaching Self-Identity, Self-Worth, and Self-Love

She will be frustrated with your thought process, your rules, and the way you run things.

CHAPTER 3

"Don't talk to me!" Developing a Strategy for Breakdowns.

There is a strong reality that there have been and will be times when you both need verbal and physical space. As a mom you will realize it is better to walk away and say nothing in the moment to calm yourself down. And for your daughter she will have the same. She will be frustrated with your thought process, your rules and the way you run things. You both will realize the space and time given are just what you need to regulate your mind and restore peace before you respond. I am including this Chapter because I believe we as mothers feel our children should never have the authority to tell us they need space or time. They sure bet not tell us "don't talk to me." As an African American mother I believe it has been ingrained to show respect and to be authoritative as a parent. Because it is not okay to have our children talking back to us in public, getting smart and making it appear as we are not in control of the situation or our children. What I am looking for and would like our Princesses to learn in this Chapter is how to respectfully create and articulate to us when emotionally they are overwhelmed. Whether it's with frustration, anger, sadness or lack of understanding. This chapter is about breaking the cycle and providing insight and depth to what is acceptable when space is needed to nonverbally communicate.

Now we have all seen this and possibly experienced it ourselves growing up. I know I was one of those adolescence who made up in my mind that I was NOT going to talk to my mom for the rest of the day because I had just gotten into the worst of trouble! For some reason I just knew my NOT talking to her was going to hurt her a lot more than it hurt me. Of course that awkward silence and walking back and forth with the biggest attitude I thought I could muster without getting into more trouble for having an attitude didn't last too long.

> *A lot of what we experience emotionally when we cannot seem to articulate what we are feeling is a breakdown. According to the Dictionary a breakdown is a failure to work or be successful. We are going to discuss when that breakdown resembles and looks a lot "like shutting down."*

When you or your child may feel "I don't have anything more to say. I will keep quiet on the matter from now on." Fully disengaging and offering no words. No feedback with the expectation that they get it because of your silence and nonverbal attitude. Arms folded, a piercing stare that could kill, head tilted to the side. It could be a verbal all out tantrum of why things are not going just the way they should. Letting the other know, I don't have anything to say and ignoring the situation and the person. Building a wall of resentment, confusion and making it harder to effectively communicate with your Princess.

How do you feel when you are not in control? How do you allow yourself to be vulnerable?

(*Vulnerable def*: Someone who is completely and rawly open, unguarded with their heart, mind, and soul)

_____

_____

_____

_____

_____

Tessa Thompson

AS AN ADOLESCENT MY DAUGHTER EXPERIENCED BREAKDOWNS AS SHE BEGAN TO DISCOVER SELF-IDENTITY. We will talk more about self-identity in chapter 5, but for now self-identity in recognizing her qualities as an individual in relation to our home and outside influences such as school and friends. Trying to understand who she looks the most like, who loves her, how she is vocal about her needs, likes, and wants, who doesn't like her and how she fits in to be most like those around her has caused tremendous breakdowns. Breakdowns for her consisted primarily in the classroom and school environment beginning at school age of four years. Most recently it has carried over into our home environment. We have experienced a breakdown at its extreme with her totally removing herself from the situation and running away. Running away at first included attending school while she was on the run and when the behaviors caused her to be suspended more and placed outside of her home school she stopped attending school altogether. When a child is outside of your home it creates a greater barrier to keep consistent and healthy communication. When she was home because of her behaviors in the community and school it was very difficult to be able to keep our home life separate because she would receive the natural consequences of her choices. Therefore, it diminished the opportunity for one on one time. It became difficult to talk to her because of her behavior. I could tell that resentment was easily setting in for me. I began to believe she was unappreciative of my love, values, and qualities I was trying to instill in her. I would take her breakdowns and behavior personally. I knew her behaviors were not who I was raising her to be and would be appalled and embarrassed by her acting out.

In a developmental period where emotions are impulsive and one track minded it becomes difficult to see through a clouded vision. I am a strong believer that your actual perception is the reality in which you live. Oftentimes trying to convince a person no matter who they are of the opposite creates a strong barrier. You begin to have a "I don't care attitude and an "it is what it is" stance to get your point across. As a mother it then ends with you being authoritative and controlling the situation because you KNOW what is best.

In what ways have you been an authoritative parent?

_____

_____

_____

_____

_____

_____

_____

_____

_____

_____

WHAT HAS WORKED FOR US OVER THE LAST ELEVEN YEARS HAS BEEN A LOT OF, TRYING NEW THINGS AND BEING OPEN TO OTHERS VOICE AND GUIDANCE. I have sought counseling for my daughter, and most recently for myself. She has attended one on one counseling, intensive outpatient treatment, individualized education planning, in home therapy as a family, and community-based programming as a family in a fun and creative way. Each of these outside services provided a different tone and perspective for me in the home. I learned to not take her breakdown and behaviors personally. I learned that a process of her self-identity and what she was experiencing was in a lot of ways a normal developmental process. What mattered the most was the unconditional love and the experiences and strategies she received while in the process. I began to fully rely on the scripture found in Proverbs 22:6 "Train a child in the way he should go and when he is older he will not depart from it." It released me from being so caught up in the moment of the breakdown and the behavior to focus more on the values of her self-identity and what I wanted her to learn and value. We began to do things like journal back and forth, write out thought processes of what she was experiencing. We would talk about the antecedents, behavior and consequences from her experiences and reality. We talked about her day, things that were funny, things that were sad. Writing became a release for her. It didn't extinguish the behaviors, but it created an area of peace for both of us.

Perhaps you are in a process of not knowing what to do in a breakdown with your Princess. Feeling like you have tried everything you know to try. Wondering if you failed at some point. Should have gotten more help or thinking only if someone else was involved. Take a moment to know not only are you enough, but you have been enough and done the best you could do as her mommy. Her current trajectory and where she is in life is not failure it is simply a moment in time. Our experiences shape us to be who we are and each moment is needed for our purpose in life. Her purpose AND fulfillment WILL BE because of what you have provided. This moment is not her lifetime so live it with optimism, with affirming faith that speaks life even if it is contrary to what you see. In the next chapter we are going to discuss the role of unconditional love and how it can provide the peace we need to strengthen ourselves as Queen.

There is a strong reality that there has been and will be times when you both need verbal and physical space.

Journal Recommendation: Developing a Breakdown Strategy.

Day 4: We are going to develop a **"Breakdown Strategy"** Openly communicate with your daughter about what a breakdown looks like for both of you Verbally and Nonverbally. **Verbally** do either of you scream? Are you quiet? Do you curse? Do you call each other names? Write it down. **Nonverbally**, do you throw things? Slam the door, leave the room or the house? Write it down.

Record your Princess' actions and feelings towards your verbal and nonverbal communication. Record your perception of what they do, their reaction to your action. Also, record how you believe they feel. Once completed use this as a discussion. If your Princess is not yet old enough to write, ask them the questions and record it. Ask her how does it make her feel when you verbally and nonverbally communicate with her. Allow your daughter to complete a journal worksheet of her own.

Verbal Breakdowns (Scream, quiet, curse)	**Non-Verbal Breakdowns** (Throw things, slam, walk away)
Reaction from Daughter: (Action & Feeling)	**Reaction from Daughter:** (Action & Feeling)

Discussion Points:

> Is my perception correct about my daughter's reaction?

> Is there anything I should change about my verbal and nonverbal communication?

> How will I work to be intentional to check in with my daughter to ensure she feels emotionally, mentally and physically safe when we are communicating whether verbally or nonverbally?

Teaching Self-Identity, Self-Worth, and Self-Love

We are going to develop a **Breakdown Strategy**. Openly communicate with your mother about what a breakdown looks like for both of you Verbally and Nonverbally. Verbally do either of you scream? Are you quiet? Do you curse? Do you call each other names? Write it down. Nonverbally, do you throw things? Slam the door, leave the room or the house?

Verbal Breakdowns (Scream, quiet, curse)	**Non-Verbal Breakdowns** (Throw things, slam, walk away)
Reaction from Mother: (Action & Feeling)	**Reaction from Mother:** (Action & Feeling)

Discussion Points:

Is my perception correct about my mother's reaction?

Is there anything I should change about my verbal and nonverbal communication?

How will I work to be intentional to check in with my mother to ensure I feel emotionally, mentally and physically safe when we are communicating whether verbally or nonverbally?

Teaching Self-Identity, Self-Worth, and Self-Love

Journal Recommendation: Developing a Breakdown Strategy

Day 5: Determining the size of the breakdown and the problem at hand can offer a perspective on how to handle it. Again, our perspective is our reality, but we have to learn to ask ourselves in relation to what? Is our reaction appropriate to the situation? Sometimes it is appropriate to offer space and time to each other. If you are experiencing a huge problem on a scale of 5 this is not an appropriate time to solve the problem or move past the breakdown. Offer a respective space to your child as well as yourself and work on another small task. Determine to revisit when you have de-escalated your emotions and feel sensible enough to talk or move forward in a calm manner.

Discuss with your Princess a **"Size of the Problem Chart."** On a Scale of 1-5 write out what a problem would look like in each area. What would the breakdown look like in relation to each number? Find a place to display it in your home so each of you can visibly see it when completed.

HOW BIG IS MY PROBLEM

1	No real problem	🙂	Happy, Calm, Relaxed
2	Having to wait, take turns, or share	🙁	Uncomfortable, Disappointed
3	Receiving consequences for unexpected behaviors	😟	Irritated, Nervous Sad, Disappointed
4	Being talked about	😢 😠	Crying, Frustrated Very Mad
5	Emergency, Tragedy, Danger	😨	Crying uncontrollably Very upset, Scared

Teaching Self-Identity, Self-Worth, and Self-Love

Journal Recommendation: Developing a Breakdown Strategy

"Size of the Problem Chart." On a Scale of 1-5 write out what a problem would look like in each area. What would the breakdown look like in relation to each number? Find a place to display it in your home so each of you can visibly see it when completed.

HOW BIG IS MY PROBLEM

1		🙂 Happy, Calm, Relaxed
2		🙁 Uncomfortable, Disappointed
3		😟 Irritated, Nervous Sad, Disappointed
4		😢 Crying, Frustrated 😠 Very Mad
5		😱 Crying uncontrollably Very upset, Scared

Teaching Self-Identity, Self-Worth, and Self-Love

Journal Assignment: Developing a Breakdown Strategy

Day 6: Have you ever noticed how you breathe when you are emotionally, mentally, or physically frustrated, angry, or distressed? You may notice fast paced breathing, increased heart rate, and an inability to find peace. Finding a how-to during these moments can bring a sense of calm and allow you to find relaxation. Breathing exercises are easy to learn and you can do them whenever and wherever you want. Practicing being intentional even one-minute brings your body, mind and emotions to a calm place by signaling your brain to relax.

Let's practice this **Royalty Breathing Exercise** together. Trace the crown.

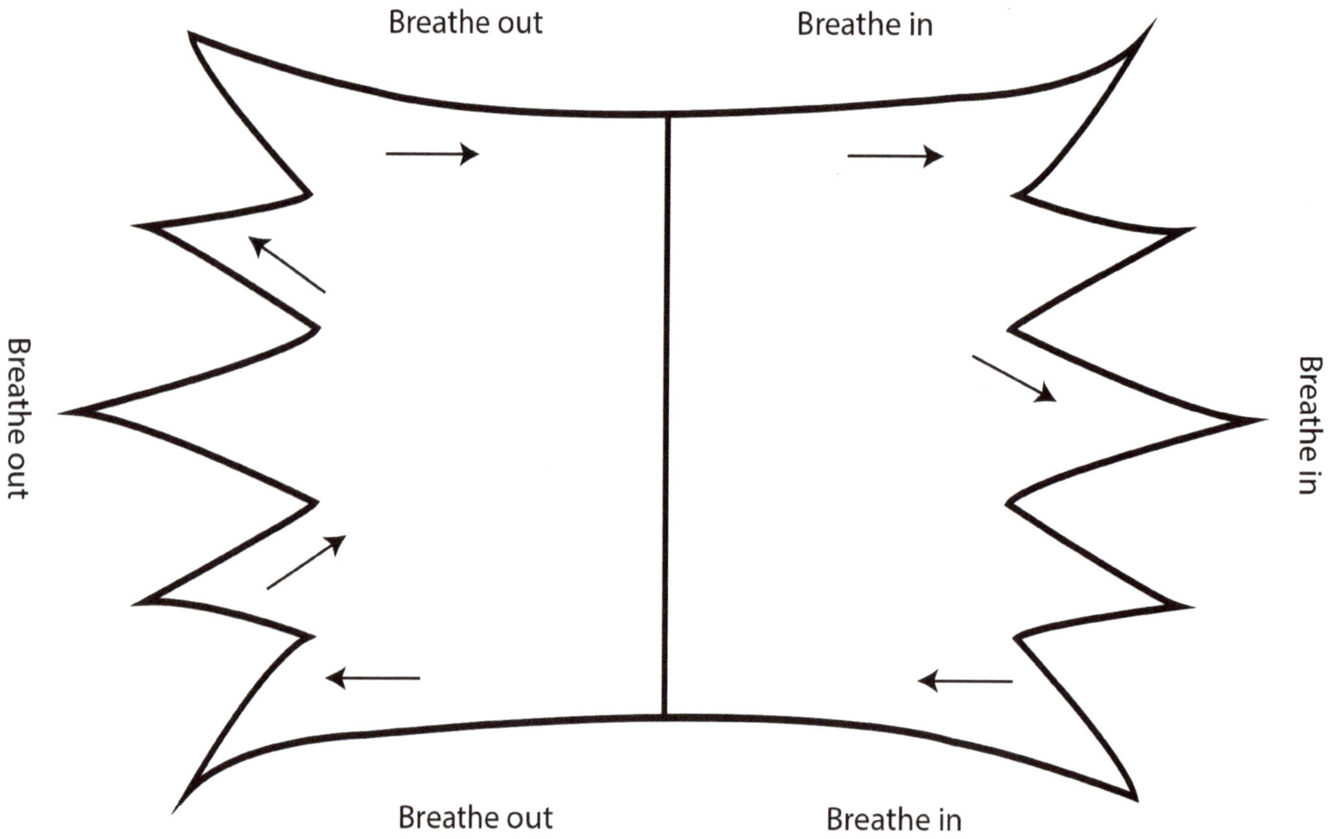

Teaching Self-Identity, Self-Worth, and Self-Love

Our response and reaction whether negative or positive reinforces her behavior.

CHAPTER 4

"Mommy still loves you." The role of unconditional love.

Being a mommy is a relentless, wonderful, and life-changing journey. From the time we find out the amount of weeks we are, to meeting our little Princess, through young adulthood. We begin to feel a sense of what love really is in its human form. We learn the love we have given them in one single decision was sacrificial in its nature to transform our lives. This affection without any limitations and love without condition, is unconditional love.

I have included this chapter because I realize life has many moments of transition and often difficulty. From birth through adolescence, teenage years and adulthood our Princess navigates her way with our direction. How she is treated with her life decision cultivates strength and empowerment or degrades her to a lack of confidence. As she is figuring out how to answer life questions and respond to different situations she must be confident she will not be confronted with scolding, reprimanding or being told how dumb she is. She should meet you with patience, taking many deep breaths and offering repeated guidance throughout this time. When we show we can be patient, consistently loving, and present it creates a secure attachment for her. A lot of times we are not aware that our response and reaction whether negative or positive reinforces her behavior.

You will find naturally your Princess is deeply hurt when she has done something to make you disappointed. She wants to please you and make you happy with her choices. You see the beam on her face and the smile from ear to ear when you notice how nicely she has done her school work, a great achievement, or how she has helped you with a task. Oftentimes she may tell you of an event that happened at school or during the day and your reply in your haste "Oh really?" "That sounds good" or "I am sorry to hear that." And you may not offer much more dialogue. Listen for ways you can help improve the situation, but not solve the problem. Offer feedback and perspective taking for your Princess to learn and grow from. Use phrases such as "What do you think?" "How do you feel about that?" or "What would you do?" Your comfort and attentive ear will draw her close. Creating an equal balance of love and perspective taking in the situation will give her the confidence to communicate with you more.

What is an example of how you can help improve your Princesses situation, but not solve the problem?

Tessa Thompson

WORDS ARE A POWERFUL WAY TO COMMUNICATE LOVE. Develop a love affirmation with your daughter. Say the short poem or prayer when the two of you re-engage following a consequence that is needed for behaviors. For example: "I am loved no matter what my behaviors are. I am learning how to make better choices and be my best self." When working to foster open communication with your Princess it is important she knows no matter her choice or decision your love is not going anywhere. She can tell because you don't yell and say how bad she is, you call it a bad choice. Learning to separate the behavior from the child builds up her self-love and provides her with a way to learn in a calm, stress free and loving environment. You will grow more confident in your approach as she learns more about your reaction and begins to communicate with you more when things aren't going 'just right.' Such as when she makes a mistake and wonders what she should do. This will be your confirmation there are no barriers or fear and she is comfortable. If over time you notice your Princess no longer comes and talks to you about the mistake she made because "I thought you would be mad at me." You should wonder what is the 'mad.' What is the verbal and nonverbal reaction she receives? Make it a precedence to go back to those love affirmations and have a conversation with your Princess, journal you and her response and utilize it as a seed and keep growing.

> *On 07/06/2017 I journaled a conversation I had with my then 11-year-old daughter who was consistently getting in trouble for her behavior at school. Everyday my husband had to go to school and I was being called on the phone. It became so bad I would begin to have panic attacks anytime I would see the school's phone number. She was being suspended or sent home at least twice a week. In that journal entry I discussed with her my love for her, that she was my first baby girl and the meaning of her name. I wanted her to always be aware of the love I had for her and how it was different than all the others love. I ended the entry with discussion of a daunting question and conversation she had long been harboring. In the midst of the school social worker and a teacher from her school she asked, "Can we keep what happens at school at school and what happens at home separate?" I am unsure if she thought I would give a different response in the presence of others or if she felt more confident by their presence. But what I did know was that she knew there was a balance provided in our home to include love and consequences. At this time her heart was merely set on just receiving the love.*

For a child who is consistently making bad choices and seemingly not learning from patient and loving correction it can be a very stressful and overbearing time period as a mom. Learning to reduce our stress and the expectation to meet the mark in the moment is often difficult. I have learned to put down the invisible cape of being "super mom" who can handle and take care of all things. And I have picked up my crown of royalty as a Queen. A Queen realizes in order to raise a Princess she must effectively take care of herself and the rest of her responsibilities. It includes finding balance. Soliciting support from a team you can count on is very important. Silence others criticism and opinions with people who are willing to empower you by offering their time and resources. Begin to isolate tough situations and ensure you do not view them as your life's work or tasks to solve all in one day. My challenge to you is put down your cape and pick up your crown. Find what brings you joy and practice your own self-care in the midst of the challenges you are facing. The challenges and the offensive behavior of your child are probably not going to change by tomorrow. Determine you will take advantage of your perspective and be filled with the joy of who you are. Find balance by pouring into yourself during this relentless journey.

What things are you carrying in trying to be "super mom?"

_____

_____

_____

_____

_____

_____

_____

_____

Who makes up your support system and what value do they give to you in being a mom?

Being a mommy is a relentless, wonderful, and life-changing journey.

Journal Recommendation: Unconditional Love

Day 7: When things become stressful for you and you feel an unequal balance list three things you will do to ensure your **self-care.** How will you remember to **put down your cape and pick up your crown**? Use the following affirmations as your guide: (Be sure to include one thing that does not have any monetary cost)

1. **I am** scheduling a manicure every two weeks to make sure I keep my appointment.
2. **I am** spending one day a week with a friend for an hour at the gym.
3. **I am** daily spending thirty minutes in the morning with meditation and journaling.

Teaching Self-Identity, Self-Worth, and Self-Love

Journal Recommendation: Unconditional Love

Day 8: Use the following writing prompts and conversation starters to get to the **heart of your child's love.** Keep the conversation light and positive. Talk over food or during a mommy daughter date. Allow your Princess to be the guide.

Is there anything you are afraid to tell me because of how you think I may respond?

What words would you like to hear from me more often?

What have I done for you in the past that made you feel really loved?

What could I do for you in the future that would help you feel loved?

Teaching Self-Identity, Self-Worth, and Self-Love

We can no longer say "sticks and stones may break my bones, but words will never hurt me."

CHAPTER 5

Self - Identity - How she fits in.

As a School Social Worker in a high school setting with an office right across from the lunchroom that I LOVE. I have a vast amount of opportunities to hear and discuss perception, thoughts and identity. It matters to each young lady what others are saying about the style of dress, attitude, clothing, music, and social group they have. Standing out is not the norm. In an adolescence development phase of self-identity, she wants to fit in while she is learning who she is becoming.

> *The Dictionary defines Self-Identity (noun) as the perception or recognition of one's characteristics as a particular individual, especially in relation to social context. Self-Identity is determining who you are in the midst of everyone else. How you fit in. How you don't fit in. Who and what you identify with and as.*

Self-identity is our daughters taking a look at how they are viewed in relation to everyone else. This topic is important because I am told quite frequently by other mom's how their daughter "should not care about what other people are saying or thinking about them. She has enough going on already. Just go to school and do her school work." They always say it so matter of factly and without hesitation. I am usually left with a mom who in return after I have a conversation about why this is not so easily done says to me, "well I never thought about it like that." We can no longer say "sticks and stones may break my bones, but words will never hurt me." Your Princess cares about what other people see, think and say about her. In a world where social media is at the touch of a finger, words hurt. Words are more immediate and reactive than ever before. Keeping social media and reality television separate from real life is very difficult. Having important conversations surrounding social media and what is done behind closed doors is very important. Especially when our children view so much of it and it is readily accessible to them. They begin to normalize what is seen and feel they must imitate those body and social images.

Who are some women or youth my Princesses age that are positive and would be a good role model? Celebrity? Positive person in social media?

_____

_____

_____

_____

_____

_____

_____

_____

_____

IT IS IMPORTANT TO TALK TO YOUR PRINCESS ABOUT HER SELF-IDENTITY BECAUSE SHE IS ALREADY THINKING ABOUT IT. She is already putting together in her mind her own thoughts and what she gathers to be acceptable and cool to say the least. If you are not talking to her about it she is left to her own thoughts and the social context of the environment outside of your home. But never for a minute think that she is not or has not received anything from you even if you've never said a word.

In becoming more open in your communication style and attitude with your Princess about self-identity, there are some things which would be acceptable to discuss and some things that you should probably avoid. You want to foster open-communication by allowing her to be your guide in this conversation topic. Asking open ended questions and allowing her to facilitate where the topic goes is the one you would receive more information from as well as more conversations, as she will find it "easy" to talk to you. Try to avoid telling your daughter she is not your friend. Try to avoid inserting your judgement to any friends or social group she discusses with you. Telling her to avoid a style of dress, music, or friend choice will not keep her from wanting to experiment more.

In discussing self-identity with my daughters, I let them decide based on the information and things I provide to them in the areas of self-worth and self-love. Self-Identity conversations are to reinforce what she already knows and builds her up to be confident in her assessment. Self-Identity comes in the questions such as my five and six-year-old coming home and telling me they want their hair to be straight and flat ironed because all the girls in their classroom, and school predominantly have straight, long and free flowing hair. So I affirm their qualities of their beautiful curly, brown and black hair that can have many more hairstyles and how it is very versatile. It works well when I provide her with options that would affirm her and build her up versus allowing her to assimilate and take on the identity of others. I ask her what she likes about her hair. Would she like to look on Pinterest to show me how she would like to do a different hairstyle. She then is excited and would like to show me new ways to style her hair. That doesn't stop her from wanting to have her hair flat ironed, but it also doesn't mean I have to put a perm in her hair to appease the way she is identifying in this moment.

Who and what your Princess identifies with is important. You shape those conversations and those thoughts. You are your child's first teacher in more ways than academically. She sees you as the first image of being a woman, a Queen. You are who she aspires to be. So be careful to assess how you describe and talk with her in a way that she can find her own way. Be open to not merely telling her the way but being her guide. This conversation style will build resilience in her and create a strong relationship for years to come.

Who are some women you admire?

What do you want your daughter to remember most about you as a person? How do you foster this quality in your daily living?

Self-Identity – She wants to fit in while she is learning who she is becoming.

Journal Recommendation: Self-Identity

Day 9: Self-Portrait Reflection. What words did you and your Princess use to describe your self-portrait?

What creativity did you show?

What do you love about yourself?

What does being a Princess who will become a Queen mean to you?

Teaching Self-Identity, Self-Worth, and Self-Love

Journal Recommendation: Self-Identity

Day 10: Journal with your daughter **her strengths.** For each strength has she found a passion or something she loves doing in that area? By building up her strengths and passions you build up her perception about who she is. Reinforce her resilience by being creative.

Example:

Strength:
Good Drawer

Passion:
Coloring and making Mandala's

Teaching Self-Identity, Self-Worth, and Self-Love

Journal Recommendation: Self-Identity

Day 11: Ask your daughter who is **one person in their school, community, or home life they like.** Is this person's name mentioned a new name for you? What does your Princess like about this individual? Invite them over for a play date. Learning who your Princess' friends are gives you insight and an open ear to her communication style and her likes.

Support System – Who is in your circle?

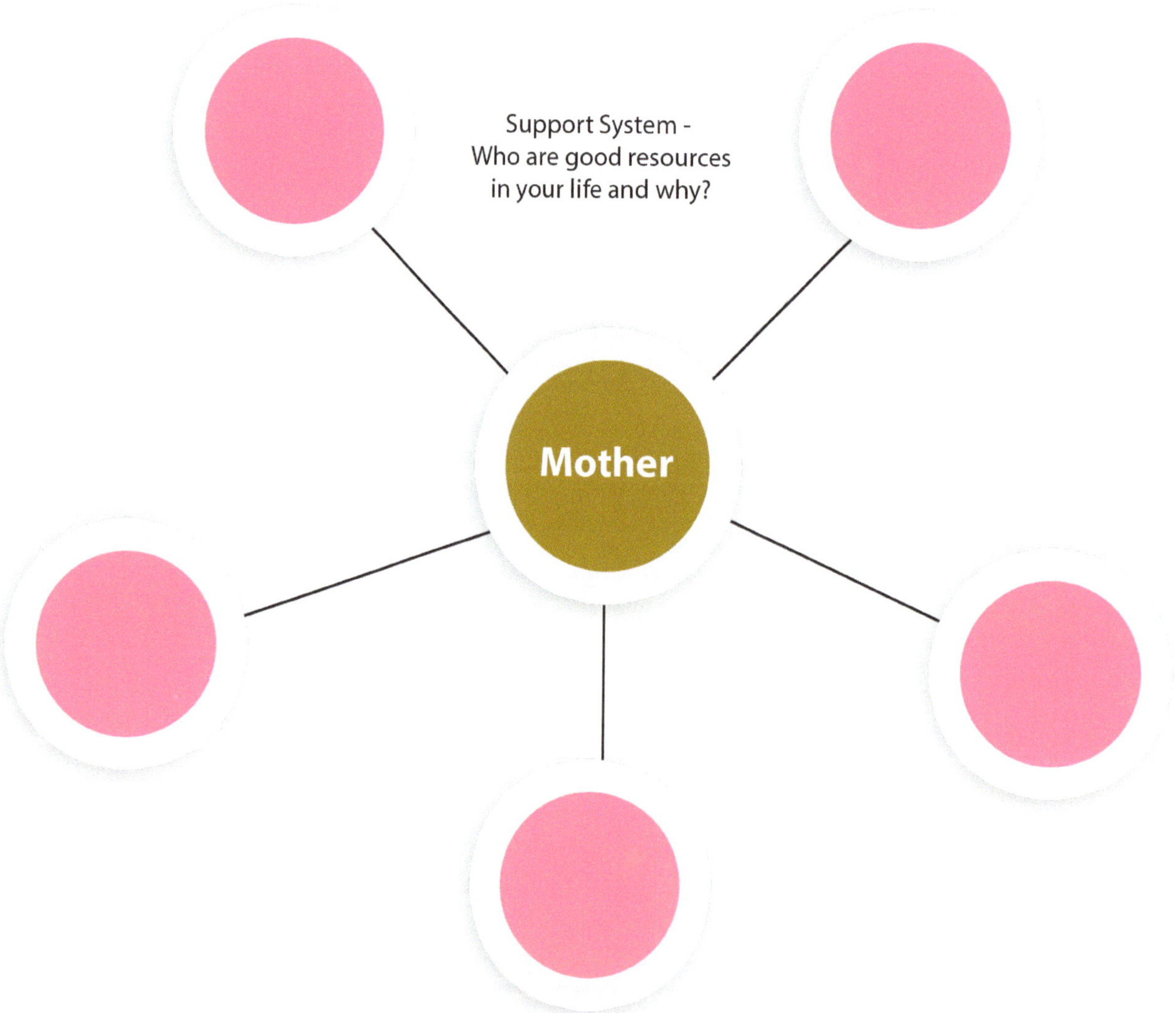

Support System - Who are good resources in your life and why?

Mother

Teaching Self-Identity, Self-Worth, and Self-Love

Journal Recommendation: Self-Identity

Day 11: Ask your daughter who is **one person in their school, community, or home life they like.** Is this person's name mentioned a new name for you? What does your Princess like about this individual? Invite them over for a play date. Learning who your Princess' friends are gives you insight and an open ear to her communication style and her likes.

Support System – Who is in your circle?

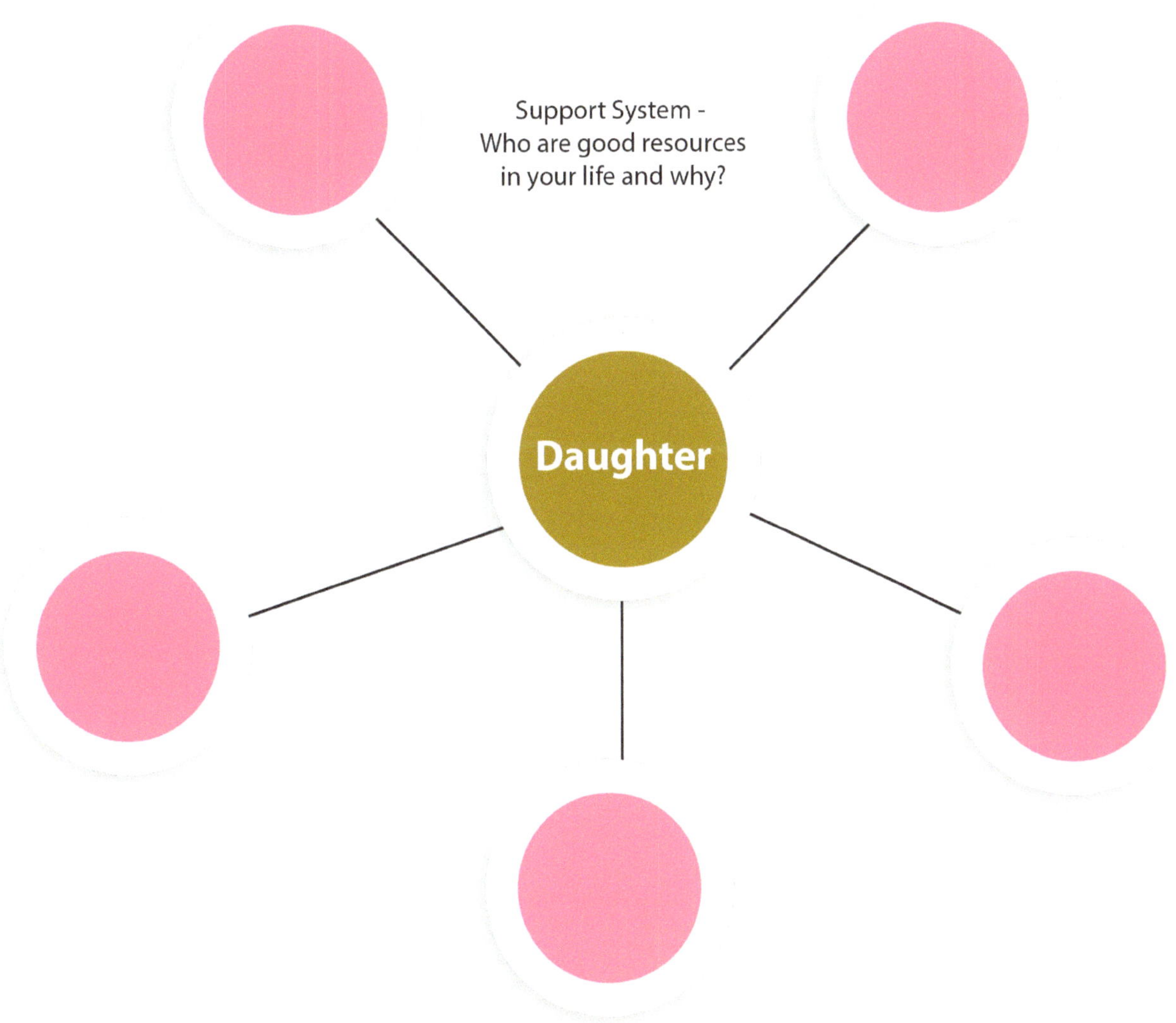

Support System - Who are good resources in your life and why?

Daughter

Teaching Self-Identity, Self-Worth, and Self-Love

*Self-Worth —
the confidence in
one's own worth
or abilities*

CHAPTER 6

Self-Worth – How she sees herself and Self-Love – Teaching "I love me" first.

My younger three children have attended a Montessori setting since the age of two. There was something that Maria Montessori figured out in early childhood learning and capacity building that I knew summed up the education I wanted for my children. She found the more children become devoted to their independence it builds their intrinsic motivation. There is a sense of pride and reward when children are allowed to work independently and self-discover. Her philosophy is "follow the child." Follow their capabilities, their independence, what they are ready for and how they *choose* to learn from the world presented to them. How often do you let this happen for your Princess?

> *The Dictionary defines Self-worth (noun) as confidence in one's own worth or abilities.*

So, when my three-year-old tells me "mommy I got it" as he confidently puts his shirt on inside out I stand by and I smile and tell him what a great job he is doing. I know it may not be done just perfectly, but I adhere to his confident nature as I know it builds his self-worth. If I tell him. "no let me do it" or diminish the opportunity for him to put his shirt on

51

inside out, I miss it. Taking control and not offering autonomous completion does not give confidence to our Princess. I get it in our busy life schedules it would take us a lot shorter time to get the clothes together on our own, wash the dishes, sweep the floor, recycle the trash, prepare a meal or other small task but the joy in their eyes and the self-worth which is produced after you make a big deal of the final result, is priceless. Perhaps you notice over time you no longer make such a big deal out of the same accomplishments because they now have it "figured out" and can successfully put on their shirt with no problem. Perhaps now that they grow older it is the task of picking out the clothes and ironing them.

When was the last time you showed your excitement in your Princess' last area of confidence and independence?

_____

_____

_____

_____

A LOT IS LOST WHEN ONE DOES NOT BELIEVE IN THEIR OWN ABILITIES BECAUSE IT HAS NOT BEEN REINFORCED OR BUILT UP. I want to ensure we never give up dreaming for our Princess, it is powerful beyond measure. It was my mother's strong vision and continued prodding when she said "I don't see that for you, Tessa, I see you in an executive role carrying out your purpose." It was her relentless yet small push that gave me permission and strength to pursue my purpose, even as an adult.

Can you recall the pivotal moment in which you made a choice to pursue your own happiness?

_____

_____

_____

When did you last share your vision for your Princess and give her permission to pursue her purpose?

Self-love — regard for one's own well-being and happiness

Self-Love – Teaching "I Love Me" First

> *The Dictionary defines Self-Love as the regard for one's own wellbeing and happiness.*

Learning to love ourselves consciously as women is something I believe we are still trying to be intentional about. Balancing our lives and proving to put self-love first is not always at the top of the list as a priority. We usually put our wellbeing and happiness following the care of home, running the kids around, providing care for extended family members, our spouses, significant others, career, and community engagements. I don't know about you, but going to get a mani and pedi can take some time to fit into my schedule. Heck shopping and doing the fun stuff can sometimes feel like a chore. I have had to get over the mom guilt and the expectation of self after returning from such stress free and joyful activities. I come home thinking about all of the things that went unattended and I find myself working hard to 'catch up.' So self-love is not always the easiest task to contribute to my total regard of peace and life joy. Some days I settle for going into my bedroom or the bathroom and unwrapping a chocolate Lindor truffle with the fudge swirl in the middle and devour its deliciousness in the moment before I have six tiny hands and three tiny voices telling me how they would really like to have some. Or perhaps it's sticking the three magnum chocolate cookie ice cream bars in the way back part of the freezer and waiting until everyone is asleep and I've been intentional to ensure I don't fall asleep and I enjoy one magnum bar as a reward to myself for having such a stand up day. That to me in finding my balance is self-love. A celebration of me everyday nothing is too small. I have learned it is intentional. This is the lesson I want us to teach ourselves first and then to our Princess.

Take a moment and list some of the things you love (I've recorded some of mine to the right).

1. _____   1. God

2. _____   2. Spouse

3. _____   3. Kids

4. _____   4. Photos

5. _____   5. The Sunrise

How long did it take for you to think or name your SELF? Self-love is intentional and if it took you awhile to name or even think of yourself it may be a sign of where your self-love is. I had to learn to take "mommy time" for myself. My life after work could not be consumed primarily with my babies. No matter how much I love them and miss them after being away from them all day. It is important that I begin to teach my daughters about balance. That even though we may not want to be away from each other, mommy must work and I also must spend some alone time with daddy by going on dates and enjoying other things in life without them being present. Intentional practices and spending time with the things that bring you personal happiness teaches your Princess you value self-worth. This is a big matter in regards to not being able to tell her to love herself and believe in her abilities and you don't believe in them for yourself. Be sure to be intentional about your "I am" self-care items listed in Chapter 5.

One of the ways to empower self-worth and self-love with your Princess is by teaching affirmations. Affirmations are positive statements that would affirm positivity. It can signify courage, strength, image or bravery. My four and six-year-old Princess' have a short affirmation that is placed in multiple places such as engraved in the back of their ipod's with their names, on their wall, in the bathroom and on the inside of their backpacks. It is: *I am brave, I am brilliant, I am beautiful.* Your discussion and reinforcement of this intentional practice builds her up. It is such an affirming word in our household that our children understand its meaning and use it to reinforce when they are scared, unsure and looking for courage. After conquering a difficult task our youngest will come up to us for a sense of accomplishment and say "Aren't you proud of me, I was so brave." What short positive phrase or affirmation can you think of with your Princess?

If you find it difficult to think of words or phrases be intentional about making a dream or vision board together. It is a collage of pictures, images, and or words placed on a poster board. You determine the size. Find inspiration in the images you collect together. I challenge you to do one with your Princess yearly as their thoughts, dreams, and vision changes as they experience life. Perhaps she is like my 6-year-old whose dream board includes all things perfume, lipstick and nail polish at this point.

Self-Worth and Self-Love are both things only you can do for yourSELF. If you are having difficulty and struggle from time to time, know that you are not alone. Determine to empower yourself by doing the things that bring you joy if even for a moment and then do it repeatedly. Enlisting a group of good #goalfriends other mamas or relatives who 'get it' will help when you are feeling overwhelmed or stressed. They can help provide the balance to get you out of the house when needed, plan a #girlstrip or grab lunch, coffee, or a run. So remember to not be so consumed that you aren't scheduling time, answering a text or phone call. Raising Royalty means you are treating yourself like the Queen you are. Never forget - you come FIRST.

A celebration of me everyday nothing is too small.

Journal Recommendation: Self-Worth & Self-Love

Day 12: What **affirmation** can you and your daughter develop together? What does it mean? Why is it important?

- I am brave
- I am bold
- I am brilliant

Teaching Self-Identity, Self-Worth, and Self-Love

Journal Recommendation: Self-Worth & Self-Love

Day 13: Develop a **dream and vision board** with your Princess and place it where you both can see it.

My Vision Board

A Dream/Vision Board is a collection of print - magazines, photos, newspaper, drawings that would bring symbolization to your goals, thoughts, and aspirations. You should be able to look at your Vision Board and be empowered to move forward no matter what adversity comes your way. Your Vision Board is a visual reminder, that YOU are always worth it!

Teaching Self-Identity, Self-Worth, and Self-Love

Journal Recommendation: Self-Worth & Self-Love

Day 14: As a mommy it can be difficult to ensure we practice perspective taking with our Princess. Today is about making an **accountability** plan with each other. Being held accountable to how we speak and listen is a valuable asset. Use the following sentence starters as a guide.

Speaking	Listening
I think _____ because	Can you explain _____
I don't understand _____	Can you tell me more about _____
_____ has been bothering me because _____	What I hear you saying is _____

We will practice self-worth and self-love by holding each other to our agreed upon communication style when speaking and talking with each other. If we get off track in our communication plan we will remind each other by:

As the speaker/listener it is okay for you to give me reminders in how I am communicating by:

Mother _____

Daughter _____

Teaching Self-Identity, Self-Worth, and Self-Love

Queens wear crowns not capes

CHAPTER 7

FINAL THOUGHTS

We have discussed how to create organic consistency in conversations that no matter the time or the place even the most difficult conversations can be had. You have developed strategies and created tools with your Princess for use when communication is difficult. You've navigated how to deal with despair, hurt, and the ugly things we don't always want to talk about. And finally, you've provided depth to the vital sense of self through self-identity, self-worth, and self-love. Your empowerment and positivity of self-affirmation is life changing.

It is my deepest desire that the Queens who are Raising Royalty have found another "how to" that empowers you on this journey. This journey has moments we are 100% confident in our abilities as mommy's and then others where we question if we are really doing the right thing. This book is to validate your journey and to remind you about the beautiful Queen in you and all of your hard work and ambition for your relationship together. The communication you have with your daughter and how the foundation is created will be here for years to come. Open communication is one that is fostered and weathered through any type of adversity, self-development, questioning or uncertainty.

As we continue on this journey together I would love to stay connected with you. You can find me on my personal website with all links to social media and blogs and other materials at www.mrstessathompson.com. Please stop by and tell me how you and your Princess have done on this journey. Never give up being the best mommy you can be. Remember to continue to practice finding balance in your life. Spirituality, Self-Care, Family, Career, and Entrepreneurship. Find the time each day to receive a little of each. Every day ensure nothing suffers more than the others. And then keep moving. YOU are the most valuable asset of royalty. Without you, you cannot raise your Princess to be the Queen she is destined to be. In finding balance it provides you with the peace that is needed to ensure you make it through your moments, your days and the future ahead. Continue to put down your cape and wear your crown proudly.

Pictured left to right (Charly Thompson, Heaven Vera, Tessa Thompson, Journey Grace and Bernadette Pendleton)

EPILOGUE

Day 1: Self-Portrait

Day 2: Pair-Share

Day 3: Journaling Schedule

Day 4: Breakdown Strategy

Day 5: Determining the size of a Problem

Day 6: Royalty Breathing

Day 7: Self-Care

Day 8: Conversation Starters

Day 9: Self-Portrait Dialogue

Day 10: Strengths & Passions

Day 11: Discovering Friendships & Support System

Day 12: Affirmations

Day 13: Dream & Vision Boards

Day 14: Accountability Partners

www.ingramcontent.com/pod-product-compliance
Lightning Source LLC
Chambersburg PA
CBHW041546220426
43665CB00002B/44